LIDLESS

BY FRANCES YA-CHU COWHIG

★

DRAMATISTS
PLAY SERVICE
INC.

LIDLESS
Copyright © 2012, Frances Ya-Chu Cowhig

All Rights Reserved

SPECIAL NOTE

The world premiere of LIDLESS was produced by the University of Texas at Austin's Department of Theatre and Dance in Austin, Texas, in 2009. It was directed by Halena Kays; the scenic design was by Jeff Jones; the lighting design was by Nathan Brittain; the dramaturgy was by Carrie Kaplan; and the stage manager was Maur Sela. The cast was as follows:

ALICE .... Kim Adams
BASHIR .... Joey LePage
RHIANNON .... Jena Kirmse
RIVA .... Sofia Ruiz
LUCAS .... Miyaka Cochrane

The European premiere of LIDLESS was produced by the High Tide Festival in Suffolk, England, in 2010. It was directed by Steven Atkinson; the 'set design was by takis; the lighting design was by Matt Prentice; the sound design was by Steve Mayo; the music was by Tom Mills; and the stage manager was Charley Sargant. The cast was as follows:

ALICE .... Penny Layden
BASHIR .... Antony Bunsee
RHIANNON / ZAKIYAH .... Greer Dale-Foulkes
RIVA .... Amber Agar
LUCAS .... Paul Blair

The New York premiere of LIDLESS was produced by Page 73 productions (Liz Jones & Asher Richelli, Executive Directors) at the Walkerspace in New York in 2011. It was directed by Tea Alagic; the set design was by Scott Bradley; the costume design was by Jessica Pabst; the lighting design was by Tyler Micoleau; the sound design was by Daniel Kluger; the dramaturgy was by Michael Walkup; and the stage manager was Shayna O'Neill. The cast was as follows:

ALICE .... Danielle Skraastad
BASHIR .... Laith Nakli
RHIANNON .... Emma Galvin
RIVA/ZAKIYAH .... Maha Chehlaoui
LUCAS .... Thom Rivera

LIDLESS was developed, in part, with assistance from the Michener Center for Writers, the Yale Drama Series, the David C. Horn Foundation, the Keene Prize for Literature, the Alley Theatre, Seattle Rep, the Ojai Playwright's Festival, the Hedgebrook Women Playwrights Festival, the High Tide Festival, the Contemporary American Theatre Festival, Interact Theatre, Marin Theatre Company, Yale Repertory Theatre, the Yaddo Colony, the MacDowell Colony, the Ragdale Foundation, and the Santa Fe Art Institute.

CAST OF CHARACTERS

ALICE, 25, then 40, white Texan

BASHIR, 48, Pakistani-Canadian

RIVA, 25, then 40, Iraqi-Assyrian Texan

LUCAS, 40, Alice's husband; racially ambiguous. Born in Northern California, moved to Texas in his teens.

RHIANNON, 14, Alice's daughter

ZAKIYAH, 22, Bashir's daughter

Note: RIVA and ZAKIYAH should be played by the same actor.

PLACE and TIME

A day in a Guantánamo Bay detention camp in 2004 and a week in Minnesota fifteen years later.

PRODUCTION NOTE

The suggested aesthetic is minimal, not realistic. Set pieces should be able to transform instantly in function and perspective. Sections should not be treated as discrete scenes, but movements that flow into one another, with areas of overlapping soundscape, movement, and image. Stage objects should be treated as if they are their own organisms, and be presented, manipulated, and allowed to breathe as such.

LIDLESS

MOVEMENT ONE

An orange shaft of light falls center stage, defining the rectangular shape of an interrogation room. An inhaler lies outside the orange light. Offstage, a girl has an asthma attack. Rhiannon enters, finds her inhaler, and breathes into it. She wears a black hoodie. Bulky headphones hug her neck. She flicks a cigarette lighter on and off.

RHIANNON. Just this one breath, just this one exhale. Just this one breath, just this one exhale. Just this one breath … *(Continues. Rhiannon places her headphones over her ears. The sound of ocean waves fills the space, morphing into white noise. Riva enters, in the uniform of a U.S. Army medic. She steps into the orange light and faces the audience.)*

RIVA. Breathe in, and out. In, and out. One more time. In, and out. Make a fist. Release. Other hand. Release. Point, then flex your feet. Lovely. *(Into recorder.)* Wrists and ankles show evidence of binding ligature injuries. Detainee complains of severe abdominal pain and should be tested for liver disease. Additional complaints include problems in respiration, likely stemming from a hood made of synthetic material repeatedly placed over the head and neck. Extensive bruising along the chest suggests internal injuries consistent with the slow, deliberate application of force. *(Riva steps out of the orange light. Alice enters, wearing a U.S. Army jacket. Her hair is wound into a bun. She steps into the orange light and faces the audience. She pulls a notebook out of the shoulder pocket on her jacket.)*

ALICE. *(Speaking with a Texas accent.)* It's the fucking U.N. out there. Nepalese food crew, Filipina launder-ladies, Ugandan guards, Ukrainian shit-cleaners. The Indians who hack grass have engineering degrees. Is my favorite meteorologist ready to tell me how he fits into this merry melting pot? I hear the families of detainees who don't cooperate run into trouble with the municipal police. It's a cold time of year to be homeless in Islamabad, don't you think? Zakiyah was, what, when you last saw her — three? Memories are fickle, my friend. One minute she'll be wondering, "When's Daddy coming home?" She'll wait by the door, her longing turning to hate each day you don't return. Then one day she won't remember you. *(Digging in.)* Who owns the house in Shekari? *(Pulls a photo out of her notebook.)* Her eyes are so bright. So hopeful. Remember when we were like that? Once upon a time I had twelve antennas on my roof. My jungle of hope. My metal arms reaching into the world. "CQ, CQ, CQ. This is Whiskey Alpha One, Little Bo Peep." I slept with an inflatable globe, tracing borders with my fingers, trying to imagine life, actual life, inside those shapes. Every symbol, every language, was a code. One I knew I could crack. I get you. I am you. According to your medical file, we even have the same blood type. *(Beat.)* Why were you in that house? Why were you in Afghanistan? Why weren't you home with your family? Zakiyah — something happens when I say her name, doesn't it? Zakiyah. Zakiyah. Why are you crying? *(Alice glances at the ceiling.)* Oh. Shit. Riva! *(Alice steps out of the orange light. Riva finds her there.)* Hey, Mama Bird, will you do me a favor?

RIVA. What you want, girl?

ALICE. Mr. B. says he sees a little girl on the ceiling. Trouble is, I see her too. What does it mean if we're having the same hallucination?

RIVA. It means you need to sleep.

ALICE. Can't. I'm too close. Just talk to me for a couple minutes 'til I find my reset.

RIVA. *(Beat.)* Did you choose a dress?

ALICE. Yeah. The strapless floor length.

RIVA. In Candlelight?

ALICE. Eggshell.

RIVA. You and Lucas better live happily ever after. I'm not getting another shirt stained by your tears and mascara.

ALICE. I'm on it. *(Alice takes a bottle of pills out of her jacket, shakes some into her hand, and offers the bottle to Riva.)* Tic-Tac?

RIVA. You're abusing those pills.

ALICE. *(Shrugs.)* Army issue.

RIVA. They're not candy.

ALICE. You wanna remember this? Suit yourself. Just don't come stainin' my shirts with your tears and mascara when you have nightmares about this shit unhappily ever after until the end of your days.

RIVA. Sweet dreams. *(Alice swallows the pills and puts the bottle in her pants pocket.)*

ALICE. Now. How do you say "needle dick" in Arabic?

RIVA. You're such a bitch.

ALICE. Cakewalker? Fudge-packer? She-goat? Fairy queen?

RIVA. The detainee speaks English.

ALICE. Aw, c'mon Riva! You trip these guys out, lookin' like their wives and daughters. Help me with this.

RIVA. I grew up in Texas. I'm Christian. I am nothing like these men.

ALICE. The chumps at 'Chuca gave me nothing for this. This isn't the Cold War. He's not a fucking Soviet spy. These guys, with their fastin' and prayin' — they can shut you out. Go anywhere in their heads. That bullshit 'bout waterboarding, the inhumanity of it all — it's missing the point. These guys believe there's a special place in heaven, with extra virgins and shit, for people who die by drowning. All you do when you waterboard is give 'em extra credit for the ever after. We gotta make 'em stop believing. Make it matter whether they live or die. What we gotta do is, damn their souls.

RIVA. You're an atheist.

ALICE. He's not. *(Beat.)* Big guy in Washington, he's figured it out. *(Hands Riva a piece of paper.)* Latest memo, from someone who's paying attention.

RIVA. *(Reading.)* "Invasion of Space by a Female"?

ALICE. A spankin' new strategy, straight from the top. "Invasion of Space by a Female." Catchy, huh? *(Alice puts her notebook in the shoulder pocket of her jacket.)*

RIVA. You'll be back in Corpus in a week. You don't have to do this.

ALICE. But I'm allowed to. Dick Cheney says so. *(Alice lets down her hair, tousles it, takes off her jacket, and adjusts her breasts. She does this in a slow, mocking striptease, and pretends to give Riva a lap dance. Chanting, seductively.)* Show me what democracy looks like, I am what democracy looks like, show me what America looks like, I am what America looks like.

RIVA. Alice. *(Giggles.)* Alice, stop. *(Alice tosses the jacket to Riva.)*

ALICE. Hold this for me.

RHIANNON. *(Reading from her notebook.)* If you were a bird, which would you be? Where would you fly for the winter?

RIVA. Not another bruise, Alice. Not a single laceration. Or I will report you. Is that clear?

ALICE. The world happens, Riva. Whether we're watching or not.

RIVA. Are we clear?

RHIANNON. What do you dream about?

ALICE. Crystal. *(Alice takes out a dark red lipstick and applies it to her lips.)* Alright, Mama Bird. Wish me luck.

RIVA. I am in the army for two things — citizenship, and a free ride to med school. You may be my best friend, but if you do anything that compromises those two things, like make another mark to his body, I will turn you in.

ALICE. I heard you the first time.

RIVA. *(Interrupting.)* Give me the lipstick.

ALICE. Sweetheart, it's not your color. *(Alice hands Riva the lipstick. Riva uncaps the lipstick and smears the dark red color all over Alice's hands.)* What are you doing?

RIVA. Tell him you're menstruating. If he thinks you're on your period — he'll go crazy.

ALICE. Mama Bird. How'd you get so smart?

RIVA. *(Affects Texas accent.)* Lived in Iraq till I was eight. *(Drops accent.)* Good luck. *(Riva exits. Alice steps into the orange light.)*

ALICE. Hey now. For a second there, with the light on you like that, you looked like my Lucas. Call me overworked and underfucked, but from where I'm standing, y'all could be cousins.

RHIANNON. If you were an infectious disease, what organ would you attack? How would you take over the body?

ALICE. I'm touching myself. My fingers trail up my thigh as I think of all our bodies could do. I could sink onto your hard, hot cock. I could bury my face in your neck. You could hold me. You could move me. You could help me find light and redemption and peace.

RHIANNON. If your life were a fairy tale, which would it be? Would you live happily ever after?

ALICE. What's the matter, Mo? Is the great Islamic sword too weary to rise today? *(Beat.)* Holy mother. Looks like I found your sweet spot. Right here. An inch beneath your left ear. Jesus. I could hang Old Glory on that pole. I've been wasting my time on white boys. It appears those rumors about Asian men are lies your ladies tell to keep you to yourselves. Selfish bitches.

RHIANNON. Is there anyone in your life you would consider to be your soul mate?

ALICE. What are we going to do about that boner? *(Alice flinches. She wipes invisible spit off her face.)* Now, now. The only spittin' allowed is the kind that comes from down there. Besides. You like this. Our heads and hearts try to trick us, but our bodies never lie. Roll with me, baby. Don't fight.

RHIANNON. What was the happiest moment of your life? What would you trade to be frozen there?

ALICE. Give it up, sweet pea. Stop your prayin'. If Allah was in Gitmo, we'd have him in solitary, so he wouldn't be able to hear you anyway. *(Beat.)* I forgot to tell you, I'm bleeding, and there's nothing shielding you from my twenty-five-year-old cunt, just red, red, red, stainin' skin already caked pus white and blue with bruises, making you the color of the flag I've sworn to protect. I've read about your hell. Your silence condemns you to that furnace fueled by the flesh of men, where walls are fire, smoke's the only shade, and the only beverage is the blood bubbling through your burning skin. Stay silent and my blood will damn your veins, so you better hope to Allah there's no such thing as eternity.

RHIANNON. What if you were a quality of light, a blood type, a dead language, a body of water, a constellation, a direction of intention, a point in space-time, a perspective on the afterlife, or an over-the-counter drug? What kind would you be, and why? *(Alice takes off her shirt, revealing a lacy red push-up bra.)*

ALICE. Last chance. *(Blackout on stage. White noise plays at full volume, morphing into the sound of waves.)*

MOVEMENT TWO

*Darkness. Rhiannon flicks her lighter on. The lights come up
in a family living room. Lucas is frosting a cake. He wears a
heavy flannel shirt rolled up to the elbows, revealing forearms
covered in tattoos of sunflowers.*

LUCAS. A light rain, the Southern Cross, a deepening toward revelation, and … some kind of painkiller.

RHIANNON. You missed point in space-time.

LUCAS. A winter night in Minnesota on your mom's fortieth birthday. *(Rhiannon tastes the frosting.)*

RHIANNON. Da-ad! You made Mom a fake cake?

LUCAS. Just because something doesn't contain processed sugar or animal products, it doesn't mean —

RHIANNON. Fake. Fake! Fake!

LUCAS. Are you sure you're my daughter?

RHIANNON. For my fifteenth birthday, I want meat. I'm talking bacon and brisket and cowboy steaks. If you even think about serving Tofurky, I swear I will disown you.

LUCAS. I have nothing against us eating meat, as long as we —

RHIANNON. Kill it, gut it, cure it, and spend every freaking moment of our life with it. Can't we pretend meat comes from Styrofoam, like normal people?

LUCAS. Rhiannon. Are you requesting a dialogue about food systems or just trying to get out of your homework?

RHIANNON. I can't interview you, Dad. Mr. Marshall says we should pick someone we don't know for our oral history project, so we aren't influenced by previous context. But what if I pick a serial killer?

LUCAS. Set the right intention, and everything will be fine.

RHIANNON. How do I know which intention's the right one?

LUCAS. How do you know when anything's right?

RHIANNON. *(Annoyed.)* My gut. *(Beat.)* But my questions won't work. If I want to understand someone, I need to dress like them, walk like them, talk like them. I need to become them.

LUCAS. So in order to understand this cake, do I need to shove it in your face? *(Rhiannon shrieks and backs away. Riva hurries in.)*

RIVA. Sorry, I was in surgery till six. *(Riva kisses Lucas on the cheek.)* Rhiannon! Come give your fairy godmama a kiss. *(Rhiannon kisses Riva on the cheek.)* Baby bird. You get taller every week! *(Rhiannon glances out the window.)*

RHIANNON. The subject has parked the car and is approaching the front door. *(Rhiannon grabs an inflatable globe from her pocket and blows it up frantically. Lucas puts the finishing touches on the cake.)*

LUCAS. She's looking for her key. She found it. She's turning the lock, in five, four, three, two — *(Rhiannon and Riva hide, taking the cake with them. Alice enters. Her Texas accent is gone.)* Hey, lady. I see you pillaged the greenhouse.

ALICE. Your new hybrid's making me weak in the knees. What's your secret?

LUCAS. Brew one pound of worm castings with water, molasses, seaweed extract, and liquid fish. Aerate for twelve hours, preferably during a full moon, and bingo! One billion critters per teaspoon.

ALICE. Oooh, baby. I love it when you talk dirty.

LUCAS. *(Stalling.)* I heard our interview on *Garden Talk.*

ALICE. Ugh.

LUCAS. I think you have a sexy radio voice.

ALICE. I think I sound like a Muppet. *(Rhiannon and Riva emerge with the cake.)*

RHIANNON and RIVA. Surprise!!! *(Rhiannon, Lucas, and Riva sing Alice "For She's a Jolly Good Fellow." Rhiannon breathes into her inhaler. She hands Alice the inflated globe.)* Happy birthday!

ALICE. My old globe! I haven't seen that thing since high school.

RHIANNON. It has writing on it. *(Reads earnestly, like it is a foreign language.)* "Secalp eseht lla wonk lliw I dlo ma I erofeb. Ebolg ym si siht. Ecila si eman ym."

ALICE. It's written backwards. It says: "My name is Alice. This is my globe. Before I am old I will know all these places."

RIVA. One night in fifth grade your mother made all the girls at her sleepover put on lipstick, close their eyes and kiss the world.

ALICE. Wherever your lips landed marked the spot where / your true love lay waiting.

RIVA. *(Simultaneously from / .)* You'd lose your virginity.

RHIANNON. What?

ALICE. Riva. We were eleven.

RHIANNON. Mom. Now that you're over the hill, will you tell me about your time in the army?

ALICE. What does turning forty have to do with anything?

RHIANNON. Mr. Marshall said that sometimes we aren't able to talk about things until we have enough distance.

LUCAS. You said you have to interview someone you don't know.

RHIANNON. Fifteen years is enough distance.

ALICE. Baby, you're not old enough —

RHIANNON. That's what you always say.

ALICE. My gear's in the attic. How about you —

RHIANNON. Play dress-up? Have a tea party?

ALICE. See if it answers any of your questions.

LUCAS. I'd stay out of the attic. I hear it's haunted by murderous dust bunnies that eat asthmatic teenagers for breakfast.

RIVA. Wouldn't you rather go out with your aunt Riva for some double-bacon cheeseburgers?

RHIANNON. What's the big deal? Why won't you talk?

ALICE. It was another life.

RHIANNON. One I want to know about.

LUCAS. Rhiannon. That's enough.

RIVA. Baby bird, you know how my family fled Iraq when I was eight?

RHIANNON. So?

RIVA. It's hard to focus on the present when you're thinking about the past. I see this in my relatives who were older and didn't know how to forget. They are trapped in their heads.

RHIANNON. How?

RIVA. My mother only leaves the house at night. She never answers the phone or door, because she thinks Saddam's men have followed her to south Texas.

RHIANNON. But I just want to know —

LUCAS. *(Interrupting.)* Sweetheart. It's your mother's birthday. Let's celebrate her, okay?

RHIANNON. Knowing her better is a way to —

RIVA. *(Interrupting.)* Hey, Birthday Girl.

ALICE. Yes, Riva?

RIVA. Make a wish. *(Reluctantly, Rhiannon flicks the lighter on and holds it over the cake. Alice closes her eyes and blows out the flame. When she opens her eyes, Lucas, Riva, and Rhiannon are gone and she is in the florist's shop, where Bashir stands before her.)*

MOVEMENT THREE

A florist's shop. Alice is removing thorns from a stack of yellow roses. Bashir stands before her.

BASHIR. My mother had a rose garden, on the roof of our apartment in Ontario.

ALICE. Is that right?

BASHIR. In Pakistan she had mazes of roses, with three gardeners to help — but in Toronto, it was just her. She gardened in downpours. She gardened in three feet of snow. That rooftop, with those roses, was the only country she believed in.

ALICE. Can I help you?

BASHIR. *(Friendly.)* I want to buy some flowers.

ALICE. You've come to the right place. How did you hear about the shop?

BASHIR. I was driving around in my taxi, and I heard you on the radio.

ALICE. No kidding. That just aired yesterday.

BASHIR. When you gave the address to this shop, I thought — why not?

ALICE. Well, thank you for taking a risk and trying something new. I hope I have what you're looking for.

BASHIR. Me too.

ALICE. So. What's the occasion?

BASHIR. A reunion.

ALICE. Is it romantic?

BASHIR. When you close my eyes, I see her, and if I open them — she's still there. Her smell, her voice, her breath — nothing's left me.

ALICE. Oh, sweetheart. Sounds like you're lovesick

BASHIR. *(Confiding.)* People should not be allowed to haunt other people. There should be an erase button in our brains that allows each person one chance to start over.

ALICE. You can't go wrong with yellow roses. They've always been my favorite.

15

BASHIR. I'll take twelve. *(Alice builds the bouquet. She wraps the stems in a black plastic bag.)* What do I owe you?

ALICE. Twenty even. *(Bashir hands Alice a bill. Alice gives him the flowers.)*

BASHIR. Why are yellow roses your favorite?

ALICE. Pink and red are romantic. Yellow is sunny. Hopeful.

BASHIR. It's not because of that song?

ALICE. What song?

BASHIR. The one about the yellow rose from Texas.

ALICE. I never made the connection.

BASHIR. A light-skinned black woman is kidnapped by a Mexican general. While his pants are down, Texas secures its independence, and the woman becomes a hero for letting herself be raped so Texas could be won, and for two hundred years she's glorified through a song that keeps changing. She's slowly edited out until there is no memory of her race, or her rape. All that's left are her eyes, which "sparkle like diamonds."

ALICE. Thanks for the story.

BASHIR. I have another.

ALICE. I should get back to work.

BASHIR. It's from the Book of Revelation. It's about the judgment of a harlot with whom the kings of Earth have committed fornication and the dwellers of Earth have become drunk. The whore sits on a scarlet beast with seven heads and ten horns, drunk with the blood of saints and martyrs. She looks a lot like your Statue of Liberty. She looks a lot like you too.

ALICE. Anything else I can do for you?

BASHIR. Remember me. *(Bashir hands Alice a printout.)*

ALICE. What, is this some kind of resort?

BASHIR. It's a satellite photograph of Guantánamo, taken a month ago. The base is still there, but the prison's gone. Now it's swimming pools and palm trees. A maximum security Disneyland. There's a carousel where my cage used to be.

ALICE. You were at Gitmo?

BASHIR. You were my Echo.

ALICE. Sorry, guy. You got the wrong lady.

BASHIR. Is your name Alice?

ALICE. It's a common name.

BASHIR. Are you from south Texas? Do you smoke Parliaments? Are there moles along your collarbone spaced like Orion's Belt?

16

Do you wash with Ivory soap? Chew cinnamon gum? Bite your fingernails until they bleed? Is there a birthmark, shaped like a raven, an inch beneath your left breast?

ALICE. *(Laughing.)* How much did Rhiannon pay you to say that? Was Lucas in on it too?

BASHIR. My name is Bashir. You know me as detainee number one-seven-six, arrested in Afghanistan in 2001 then sent to Guantánamo, where I stayed until I was released eight years later to Canada, the country of my teenage years, because Pakistan, the country of my birth, refused to repatriate me.

ALICE. I'm a florist.

BASHIR. Hitler was an animal-rights activist. *(Offering the bouquet.)* Take the flowers.

ALICE. You want your money back?

BASHIR. I want a lot of things back. *(Screams.)* Take the flowers! *(Alice twists Bashir's arm behind his back.)*

ALICE. When I release you, you will walk out that door and never look back. Got that?

BASHIR. I got hepatitis in Guantánamo. It went untreated on your watch. I've been on a transplant list for ten years.

ALICE. Got that?

BASHIR. We have the same blood type. AB negative. You told me that during one of our "meetings." Give me your liver. Redeem yourself. Save me. *(Alice releases Bashir. He falls to the ground.)*

ALICE. My liver? You want my liver? *(Bashir hears a woman singing. He looks at Alice and sees his wife.)*

BASHIR. Shemayah. You found me. Did you get my messages? I sent thousands. There were so many birds in Cuba. Some so small they could fly into my cage. Each time a bird came to me, I gave it a message to bring to you. I told it how to find you. What winds to take. Didn't you get my messages? Why wouldn't you wait? *(Bashir reaches for Alice's hands. Whenever his arms are at full extension, his hands flutter slightly at the wrist. As soon as he touches Alice, he jolts away. The music stops.)* There's a strange light in here. A very strange light.

ALICE. You drove here, from Canada, to ask for my liver?

BASHIR. Just half. The liver regenerates. Both halves become wholes. I'm dying. I have a few months left.

ALICE. Get out of my shop.

BASHIR. More life. That's all I want. More life. I'm staying at the Motel 6. Room 124. I'll wait there until you remember me.

ALICE. That won't happen.

BASHIR. Last chance. *(Bashir waits for a moment. When Alice doesn't respond, he pulls the black plastic bag over his head, mimicking the infamous photo from Abu Ghraib. He gasps and screams and wails. He offers Alice the bouquet of yellow roses. After a moment of stillness, his extended arm flutters slightly at the wrist.)*

MOVEMENT FOUR

Hospital. Riva hurriedly changes from her street clothes into surgery scrubs. Alice stands before her. They are mid-conversation.

RIVA. No way.

ALICE. You are the only person who can help me.

RIVA. And why is that?

ALICE. I don't recognize him. I hardly remember a single thing about Gitmo.

RIVA. You didn't want to. That's why you took those pills in the first place.

ALICE. I took those pills because I grew up watching my dad wake from his 'Nam nightmares and beat the shit out of my mom. I didn't want to repeat his mistakes.

RIVA. You didn't. The pills worked. The princess lives happily ever after, like she always knew she would.

ALICE. Remember that bantam chicken you gave Rhiannon?

RIVA. Angel Wings?

ALICE. Know how she died?

RIVA. Rhiannon's pets always die.

ALICE. One night around midnight the bird started screaming. I can't remember why I pulled the first feather. It was so white, each quill tipped with blood. She didn't fight back, which made me furious. She sat on my palm, just watching, while I pulled out another feather, and another, until she was bloody and bald. I went to sleep that night feeling better than I had in years. She didn't survive the night.

RIVA. When you asked me to never talk about Gitmo, so you could "start over" and be "a good mom," I went along with it, and you know what? I love having dinner with a family whose biggest worry is what to do with the root vegetables in their CSA basket. Because I have seen — I have lived the alternative. I don't know a single Assyrian Iraqi who escaped as an adult who isn't crazy. They are crippled by their memories.

ALICE. What should I do?

RIVA. Call the cops. Turn him in. Get some therapy.

ALICE. Come with me to his motel. See if you recognize him. Please?

RIVA. You guys are my family. I moved to Minnesota to be close to you. Don't mess up your life because you turned forty and got curious.

ALICE. Don't mess up my life, or don't mess up yours?

RIVA. Alice. He's crazy! *(Riva starts to exit.)*

ALICE. What happened to your father?

RIVA. What?

ALICE. We've been friends for thirty years, and whenever I ask about your dad, you change the subject.

RIVA. That conversation is off limits.

ALICE. For me the army was a way out of Texas and into the world. For you it was different.

RIVA. Different how?

ALICE. It was personal. I remember the day at Texas State when a video of Saddam's execution showed up on YouTube. How many thousands of times would you say you watched it?

RIVA. Right. It was personal for me, which is why the minute you got permission to give a Muslim man a lap dance, you did.

ALICE. A lap dance?

RIVA. You had a week left in Gitmo. You could have ignored the memo, laid low, and been done with the army.

ALICE. What memo?

RIVA. The one that gave you ladies permission to "Be All You Could Be."

ALICE. Riva. Be specific. I really don't remember.

RIVA. For a while the interrogators looked like the rest of us, then the women started dressing up. First time I saw a girl like that, with her makeup done, her hair all blow-dried, I thought she was going on a date. She even had perfume on. I felt like I was back at Texas State, walking down Sorority Row. It was amazing how easily a bunch of women could pull off their shirts and shake their tits in search of something someone called truth. *(Riva walks away. Alice touches a spot on her ribcage, an inch beneath her left breast. She exits. In another room, Riva puts on lipstick, lost in thought. She remembers something, looks at the lipstick, then touches it to her hand.)*

MOVEMENT FIVE

The florist's shop. Rhiannon scribbles in a notebook while working the counter.

RHIANNON. "Where are you from?" Lame. "Where do you wish you were from?" Better. "If you were going to design an avatar, what would it look like? Would you be the same race, age, sex, and species? If the Tower of Babel hadn't fallen and Pangaea had never split up, who would you brunch with on Sundays?" *(Bashir enters, carrying a package wrapped in brown paper.)* If you were an animal, which would you be?
BASHIR. An iguana.
RHIANNON. Why — *(Hiccups.)* Oh no.
BASHIR. Should I scare you?
RHIANNON. You can't. *(Hiccups.)* I have a very strong constitution.
BASHIR. My mother believed we get hiccups when our body knows something our mind doesn't understand.
RHIANNON. My dad says I get hiccups when an elf crawls up my nose and does back-handsprings down my spine. *(Hiccups.)* I think hiccups are my body's way of reminding me I'm still alive. Still breathing. My heart's still beating. *(Hiccups. Bashir lunges at Rhiannon, screaming. She shrieks. Her hiccups stop. She dissolves into giggles.)* You want roses or something?
BASHIR. I was going to leave this for Alice, but I'll come back some other time.
RHIANNON. I'll take it home tonight. *(On Bashir's hesitation.)* Do I look like a snoop? *(Bashir hands Rhiannon the package.)* I read about a man who had hiccups for a year. He shot himself in the head just to make them stop.

BASHIR. Little girls should fly kites. Play with dogs.

RHIANNON. Last month my dad caught me "suffocating" a goldfish. I'm not allowed to have another animal until I learn to value life more.

BASHIR. Seems fair.

RHIANNON. I was just holding it in my hand, watching it.

BASHIR. Watching it suffer.

RHIANNON. Watching it try to breathe. The water was right there. But it kept flopping around, gasping for breath like an idiot who can't control her own body, getting attention from random people just because she breathes differently from everyone else.

BASHIR. I used to have asthma.

RHIANNON. *(Beat.)* How'd you make it stop?

BASHIR. Imagine that every day at school a bully beats you up and steals your lunch. You can't tell the principal because that would make things worse. What do you do?

RHIANNON. Learn karate?

BASHIR. What if you handed over your lunch instead of resisting?

RHIANNON. Then the bully wins.

BASHIR. Not if you enjoy it. If you can't change the situation — change yourself. With the asthma, I made myself think: "I want this. I love this. I'm happy." My breath came back. My fear went away. Everything became okay.

RHIANNON. If you give the bully your food, you'll die of starvation.

BASHIR. I'm talking about situations where you either transform the pain into something useful or die. Or go crazy.

RHIANNON. I want this. I love this. I'm happy?

BASHIR. Try it sometime. It might save a few fish. *(Bashir starts to leave.)*

RHIANNON. Did you know that lots of goldfish aren't even orange in the wild? They're gray. Or green.

BASHIR. Natural camouflage.

RHIANNON. Orange fish get eaten.

BASHIR. Or kept as pets.

RHIANNON. My goldfish wasn't a pet. I've never had pets.

BASHIR. What makes a pet?

RHIANNON. They ask at the store if the animal's going to be a pet. If you say yes, you sign a form that says you understand your pet is a living thing that needs food and water, blah, blah, blah. If you don't sign it, it's not a pet.

BASHIR. So the animal's quality of life depends on whether you classify it pet or non-pet?

RHIANNON. There's no such thing as non-pets. They're called feeders.

BASHIR. I'm afraid to ask the number of creatures you've classified as feeder.

RHIANNON. Three rats, fourteen goldfish, seven hamsters, a guinea pig, and a couple hundred crickets.

BASHIR. No puppies?

RHIANNON. This is America, fool. Puppies go to preschool.

BASHIR. There must be a way to understand cricket song besides taking a cricket and ripping off its wings.

RHIANNON. You get me. Nobody gets me.

BASHIR. I know your type.

RHIANNON. Can I interview you for my oral history project?

BASHIR. Which history do you want?

RHIANNON. How many you got?

BASHIR. There's the history of who I am and the history of who I wanted to be.

RHIANNON. How'd you get two histories? *(Bashir puts his arm around Rhiannon and leads her down an imaginary path.)*

BASHIR. Imagine you're walking down a road lined with trees. It's straight and pleasant enough. You can see for miles. You know exactly where you're going, then suddenly — *(Bashir abruptly reorients his and Rhiannon's place on stage.)* you're somewhere else. You never saw the fork, didn't make a decision to go right or left. But everything's different.

RHIANNON. Two histories, huh?

BASHIR. Which do you want?

RHIANNON. I'm not sure. Which one's more important? *(Bashir gazes at Rhiannon, considering this. Rhiannon looks away, suddenly shy.)*

MOVEMENT SIX

The family living room. Lucas is deep in a horse-stance, doing a tai chi form. He is grounded and focused, executing very slow, fluid movements. Alice enters.

ALICE. Hey, baby. *(She kisses him.)*

LUCAS. Let me finish this form.

ALICE. Mmm. You smell like mulch ... and mint toothpaste. *(Lucas relents and returns her affection.)*

LUCAS. How was work?

ALICE. I don't want to talk.

LUCAS. When I finish this form, we can be as quiet as you want. *(Rhiannon enters with her backpack.)*

ALICE. I didn't say I wanted to be quiet. I said I didn't want to talk.

RHIANNON. Next time just tell me you don't want to talk instead of making me look for things that don't exist. Or did the dust bunnies eat your gear?

LUCAS. They get pretty hungry in the winter.

RHIANNON. I want this. I love this. I'm happy.

ALICE. Want what? Sweetheart, what do you want? *(Rhiannon is silent. She closes her eyes.)*

LUCAS. Rhiannon?

RHIANNON. Shhhh. *(Rhiannon takes a few deep breaths. A smile spreads across her face. She opens her eyes. With genuine affection.)* You guys are the best. I love you. Good night. *(Rhiannon exits.)*

LUCAS. Our daughter has just been colonized by an alien life form.

ALICE. Where's the gear?

LUCAS. I wanted us to do right by Rhiannon. I didn't want anything that might be a bad influence. That's all I could think about the day she was born.

ALICE. So, what, you put my clothes in the storage unit?

LUCAS. No. I burnt them.

ALICE. What?

LUCAS. It was part of your new leaf. Just like moving to Minnesota, opening your shop, and starting my nursery.

ALICE. But what about your leaf, Lucas? Or did you never make it to yours because you were too busy turning mine?

LUCAS. You asked me to be strong for you. For this family.

ALICE. You think burning my gear is a sign of strength?

LUCAS. Strength is refusing to go to war in the first place.

ALICE. But Lucas, Afghanistan is where the world's heroin comes from. Weren't you proud that I was off fighting for your right to shoot up?

LUCAS. I kept my part of our deal. I have never asked about your service.

ALICE. Don't you think it's been a little cramped sharing our space with two elephants?

LUCAS. No, baby. I just imagine we're on a safari.

ALICE. We've been pretending parts of our lives don't exist.

LUCAS. That would be delusional. We both know there was a time when you were a soldier and I was a junkie. That's the past. It doesn't have to haunt us.

ALICE. Lucas. You tattooed sunflowers over your track marks.

LUCAS. Would you rather make Rhiannon stare at my scars?

ALICE. Wouldn't that be more honest?

LUCAS. The scars are still here. I haven't forgotten them. But they aren't going to define me, or us, or this family.

ALICE. Did I change after Gitmo?

LUCAS. We never said this would be easy. Every day I make a decision not to get high. If I went on autopilot for a single moment — it'd be over. Controlling what I think about is the hardest thing I've ever done, but you girls are worth it, even if that means doing tai chi for the rest of my life like a fucking born-again hippie. Be here, Alice. Just be here. We can get through anything as long as we still want the same thing. Do we?

ALICE. Yes, baby. This is what I want. I want to be here. Here. No place but here. (*Lucas follows Rhiannon to her room. Alice stares at the photograph of Guantánamo. Rhiannon, in her bedroom, takes Bashir's package out of her backpack and starts to unwrap it. Lucas enters. Rhiannon hides the package.*)

RHIANNON. Hey, Dad.

LUCAS. How's the search?

RHIANNON. I found my guy. I got a sign from my gut, just like you said. But don't worry — the interview will be in a public place. Everyone will be safe.

LUCAS. I trust you, sweetheart. I trust you so much that I have a favor to ask.

RHIANNON. Does it involve watering, weeding, or aerating compost?

LUCAS. As a matter of fact, it doesn't, but if you ever feel like building your biceps, I have four bins that need turning.

RHIANNON. Make your own dirt, Dad. What's the favor?

LUCAS. Have you heard of flashbacks?

RHIANNON. It's when something from the past is happening again right in front of you.

LUCAS. They make you hurt the people you love.

RHIANNON. Mom's not having flashbacks.

LUCAS. I know you're old enough to handle just about anything, but your mother's been through some scary stuff, so how about you lay off the questions for a while?

RHIANNON. What's wrong with questions?

LUCAS. Remember when you fell off your bike and scabs formed over every scrape?

RHIANNON. So?

LUCAS. What happened when you picked your scab?

RHIANNON. What's your point?

LUCAS. Questions about your mom's past, when she's trying to recover, are like picking at your scabs before they turn into new skin.

RHIANNON. That's stupid.

LUCAS. What happened to the scabs you couldn't stop picking?

RHIANNON. Fine.

LUCAS. Promise?

RHIANNON. I promise not to ask Mom questions about her time in the army.

LUCAS. That's my girl. Don't forget, we're doing the holiday photo tomorrow.

RHIANNON. I'm not wearing a dress.

LUCAS. I like your look. I won't ask you to change. Now, if you'll excuse me, there's a Tofurky in the oven that needs my attention.

RHIANNON. Very funny.

LUCAS. I even got the kind with the smoke-flavored marinade.

RHIANNON. You can't fool me, Dad. I know my meat. (*Lucas leaves. Rhiannon unwraps the package. An orange jumpsuit falls into her lap.*)

MOVEMENT SEVEN

A motel room. Bashir is on the phone.

BASHIR. Zakiyah, this is your father. I found a liver. I'm going to live! Last month I got a letter from the Pakistani embassy — they've reinstated my citizenship, issued a formal apology. I will be home in time for your wedding. *(Beat.)* I keep dreaming about the sparrows we kept in the bamboo cages we bought from the Chinese trader. How sorry you felt for them. How we sang to them every morning. There were so many birds in Cuba. Some so small they flew into my cage, sometimes perching on my knee. It's a funny world, isn't it, Zakiyah? First it was us singing to the caged birds; then I was in the cage, and the — *(Bashir puts the phone down. Zakiyah has hung up.)* The birds were singing to me. *(Bashir extends his arms. His hands flap uncontrollably — a symptom of his liver disease, hepatic encephalopathy. There is a knock.)* Come in. *(Riva enters.)*

RIVA. My name is Riva Babani. Alice told me where you were staying.

BASHIR. You are the Iraqi medic who refused to speak Arabic.

RIVA. My English is better.

BASHIR. My business is with Alice. You are free to stay out of it.

RIVA. If you have an issue with how you were treated in Guantánamo, take it up with the government.

BASHIR. The United States government does not have the same blood type as me.

RIVA. Alice is a mother now. She has a fourteen-year-old daughter. Let her live in peace.

BASHIR. I was just talking to my daughter, Zakiyah. I haven't seen her since she was three.

RIVA. Why aren't you with her?

BASHIR. I am waiting until she can see me strong. Healthy.

RIVA. You are selfish.

BASHIR. When there were hepatitis outbreaks at Guantánamo — did you report them?

RIVA. I did my job as well as I could in an environment where a majority of the detainees wouldn't look me in the eye.

BASHIR. I have a memory of you, dressing the wound of a man in the cell next to me. He said you looked like his daughter, and asked if you would sing to him in Arabic.

RIVA. I haven't spoken Arabic since I was eight.

BASHIR. You are Iraqi, but your last name is Babani? I bet your family suffered greatly under Saddam's regime.

RIVA. Everyone did.

BASHIR. Christians more.

RIVA. We got out.

BASHIR. You must have been very young when you left Iraq. But maybe you were lucky and escaped with your whole family?

RIVA. She can't save you.

BASHIR. She damned my soul. I was a good Muslim until she came to me. She damned my soul and now — I'm dying.

RIVA. *(Long silence.)* My father was tortured in Abu Ghraib. The real Abu Ghraib. When it was Saddam's prison. Because he spoke Syriac to a soldier who asked him a question in Arabic.

BASHIR. Did it work?

RIVA. Did what work?

BASHIR. Did helping Muslim men get tortured make your father's pain go away?

RIVA. They cut off his hands and put them in a box for my mother. We never got the rest of his body. I buried his hands under an orange tree, palm to palm. Like a prayer. Like a promise.

BASHIR. What kind of promise does a little girl make to a pair of severed hands that she spends her life trying to keep? *(Bashir reaches for Riva's hands. She backs away.)*

MOVEMENT EIGHT

Bashir's motel room. Alice enters. Bashir stands in front of her, holding the bouquet of yellow roses.

ALICE. What kind of person hears a woman's voice on the radio and drives to another country to ask for her liver? Her liver. What kind of sick fuck does that?

BASHIR. What kind of sick fuck leaves the army and becomes a florist?

ALICE. I will not permit you to waltz into my shop and ruin my life. Yes, I was a soldier. An interrogator who did her job. Her job! Whatever tactics I used that resulted in your ability to recall the exact shape of a birthmark on my chest was authorized by the government of the United States of America. *(Lowers her voice.)* I do not owe you a piece of my body.

BASHIR. Don't use that voice.

ALICE. If you choose to walk into my shop and put a bag over your head, I'm allowed to use whatever voice I want with you, sugar. You think actions don't have consequences? Do you?

BASHIR. It must be a relief to be your true self again.

ALICE. Spare me the true-self bullshit. No one is anything except their situation.

BASHIR. Out of all the jobs in the world, why did you become a florist?

ALICE. It's something to do.

BASHIR. But when you're a florist, life and death is in your hands. You control how much water something gets. How much light. You decide what a weed is, and at any moment you can — *(Bashir rips a rose off a stem, drops it on the floor, and steps on it, grinding it into the ground. He waves the stem in front of him.)* Is this still a rose? No roots, no flower, no future, no past. You cut them down. You rip them from their roots and thrust them into darkness, into cold storage, for display. Contained. A symbol of some fool's fierce feeling.

ALICE. How many times a day do you wish you were back in Gitmo?

BASHIR. Why would I want to go back?

ALICE. I bet you made good friends there. People who under-stand you more than anyone else on this planet. You want to be back there, where life is simple. You don't have to decide what to wear, or eat, or do when you wake up every morning. You have a role. An identity. That's what you've really lost. You got out of prison, but you never found a new self.

BASHIR. You know nothing.

ALICE. I should get out my green wire and make you a crown with those thorns. That's what you want, isn't it? *(One by one, Bashir rips the roses off their stems and crushes them.)*

BASHIR. I want to live. I want to see my daughter. I want to smell bread and honey and the sea. I want to dine with friends, with fam-ily. I want to walk beside my brothers, beside people who knew me before I was this man, this broken body. I want to lie beside my wife and get lost in her ruby black hair while we sing each other to sleep.

ALICE. *(Long silence.)* Iguanas. That's all I remember about Gitmo. Iguanas crossing the road. I was so scared of hitting one and having to pay a fucking ten-thousand-dollar fine.

BASHIR. The iguanas were lucky. The Endangered Species Act was enforced.

ALICE. I stared at the photo you gave me. But nothing's coming back.

BASHIR. What do you want to know?

ALICE. I want you to not exist.

BASHIR. You like your new roles.

ALICE. I like my life a whole lot.

BASHIR. Americans love reinvention.

ALICE. How can I even consider giving you half my liver if I don't know what I did?

BASHIR. Then I guess you'll have to interrogate me. *(Bashir offers Alice the bouquet of stems. She accepts it.)*

MOVEMENT NINE

On the street. Riva and Rhiannon mid-conversation. Riva hands Rhiannon an army jacket. It is the one Alice wore in Guantánamo.

RHIANNON. What's this?
RIVA. Your mom's jacket.
RHIANNON. She wore it during the war?
RIVA. *(Nods.)* I'm sorry I told you not to ask questions. You're our future, Baby Bird. You need to know our past. *(Rhiannon hugs Riva, then puts on the army jacket.)*

MOVEMENT TEN

Bashir's motel room. Rhiannon and Bashir are in the middle of the oral history interview. Rhiannon wears the army jacket.

RHIANNON. Next question: If you were a bird, which would you be? Where would you fly for the winter?
BASHIR. I'd be a zunzún. It's a kind of hummingbird. It can fly through chain link.
RHIANNON. I guess I shouldn't be surprised to get a weird answer from a guy who tried to give my mom a jumpsuit.
BASHIR. You told me you weren't a snoop.
RHIANNON. I asked you if I looked like a snoop. The rest you just assumed. So. Is it a war trophy?
BASHIR. A war trophy?
RHIANNON. My grandma's house is full of them. There's the bloody flag Great-Uncle Eddie jacked from a corpse during the Battle of Okinawa, a hat made of banana leaves Grandpa Joe

brought back from Vietnam — there's stuff from every family member except my mom. I bet you worked with her in the army and took that jumpsuit as a souvenir.

BASHIR. I did spend time with detainees.

RHIANNON. The guys in jumpsuits?

BASHIR. The orange fish.

RHIANNON. In pictures they look more like flies with those black things over their eyes.

BASHIR. Blackout goggles. It's just a diving mask covered in duct tape.

RHIANNON. I have a diving mask. And duct tape.

BASHIR. Then you can make one too.

RHIANNON. What would I do with that?

BASHIR. You might be surprised by what you see.

RHIANNON. Are you talking about hallucinations?

BASHIR. Close your eyes. *(Rhiannon hesitates, then closes her eyes.)* Imagine it's daylight. You feel the sun burning your face and sweat soaking your clothes, but all you see is black. Eventually your mind fills in what's missing. Maybe first it shows you the sun, then moves on to the things you really want to see.

RHIANNON. Like what?

BASHIR. The face of someone you love. You might remember an afternoon you spent making sand castles with your sister, because Gitmo is by the water, and the wind carries the spray to your face. When you can't see, everything is only what you make it. A chain around your wrist can be the hand of your wife, stale bread the cake you shared at your wedding. Moans and screams can be wind whistling through trees, and people around you can be enemies or brothers, depending on what you need to see.

RHIANNON. *(Opens her eyes.)* Why'd you want to be an iguana?

BASHIR. The iguana has cells that, when activated by trauma, can regenerate a new tail completely. It doesn't have to ask anyone for help. It just lies on a warm rock and mends.

RHIANNON. Close your eyes. *(Bashir hesitates.)* Please? *(Bashir closes his eyes. Rhiannon kisses him on the lips. He recoils.)* Oh my God. I thought — I'm stupid. I'm so stupid.

BASHIR. It's my fault. I shouldn't have let you come here.

RHIANNON. I feel like I've known you my whole life. I don't need to use my inhaler when I'm with you. I can just breathe and be myself. You don't think I'm a freak.

BASHIR. You're not a freak.

RHIANNON. Sometimes I like killing crickets. Sometimes I think it's funny.

BASHIR. You just want to understand how they sing.

RHIANNON. Stop that.

BASHIR. Stop what?

RHIANNON. You're holding your breath so that nothing affects you. Take a deep breath. I dare you. *(Bashir struggles through a long, deep breath. Rhiannon's eyes fill with tears. She exits the motel room.)*

MOVEMENT ELEVEN

The family living room. Lucas points a tripod with a digital camera mounted on it toward Alice and Rhiannon. They hold the inflated globe between them.

LUCAS. Sweetheart, move toward your mother. Alice, put your arm around Rhiannon. *(Lucas presses the timer button and hurries to join the pose.)*

ALL. Cheese! *(The camera flashes. Lucas checks the camera screen.)*

LUCAS. Alice, your eyes were closed. Let's try again.

ALICE. *(To Rhiannon.)* Let's see your whole face for the photo, 'kay, babe? *(Alice slides Rhiannon's hoodie off her head and smooths out her hair. As she does so, she catches a glimpse of what Rhiannon is wearing underneath.)*

RHIANNON. Mom!

LUCAS. Big smiles, guys. Happy thoughts. *(Lucas presses the timer and joins the group pose. The camera flashes again. Lucas checks the camera screen.)* Rhiannon, take your hoodie off for this last shot? You're looking a little blobbish.

RHIANNON. You said I didn't have to change.

ALICE. Let her wear what she wants.

LUCAS. I'm not asking you to change. I'm asking you to remove a layer.

ALICE. Let's take a break.

LUCAS. Everything's set up. It's one photo. Please don't make this a big deal. *(Rhiannon takes off the hoodie, revealing that she is wearing Alice's army jacket underneath.)* Where did you get that?

RHIANNON. Riva gave it to me when we went out for meat. She said it might help me with my homework.

ALICE. Does it? *(Rhiannon pulls the memo out of the shoulder pocket.)*

RHIANNON. *(Pointedly addressing her father.)* Hey, Dad. What's "Invasion of Space by a Female"?

LUCAS. It's what happens when you get married.

ALICE. Lucas. Don't joke.

LUCAS. Rhiannon, lose the jacket. We're taking this picture. *(Rhiannon grabs the camera and points it at her parents.)*

RHIANNON. I'll take the photo, Dad. You can Photoshop me in later.

LUCAS. Give me the camera.

RHIANNON. Come on, guys, get close. Show me those pearly whites. *(Lucas grabs the camera and rips the jacket off Rhiannon, leaving her topless except for a red sports bra.)*

ALICE. Lucas, stop! *(Rhiannon walks to her backpack, and pulls out the jumpsuit. As she speaks, she manipulates it like a puppet.)*

RHIANNON. Ladies and gentlemen, what do we have here? Why, it's a genuine, bona fide jumpsuit, straight from the land of Cuba. It's got no pockets, a double zipper, and the brand name's Prince. Kiss the right chicks while you're wearing this, boys, and you just might live happily ever after.

LUCAS. Alice. Where did she get that?

RHIANNON. Mr. Jones, tell me. Why did a man bring this to your lady's shop? Is it a souvenir? A memento? Some kind of war trophy?

ALICE. Baby, please. Talk to me. *(Rhiannon breathes into her inhaler and holds it out to Lucas, like a reporter waiting for an answer. Alice watches silently, still holding the inflated globe.)*

LUCAS. I love you. So much. Why are you doing this?

RHIANNON. Because you told me not to ask Mom any questions.

ALICE. What?

RHIANNON. Put on the jumpsuit.

LUCAS. This isn't dress-up.

RHIANNON. You wore war clothes when we went to Gettysburg. We were even on opposite sides.

33

LUCAS. Remember when we talked about boundary violations? Wearing that jumpsuit would be a violation of my boundaries.

RHIANNON. I'd wear it.

LUCAS. That's the beautiful thing about boundaries. There's nothing wrong or right about where we put them.

RHIANNON. What if my boundary ends in your stomach? Do you have to respect my fist in your stomach because I say it feels great?

LUCAS. If punching me will make you feel better, then please, hit me.

RHIANNON. Have you ever felt like you've known someone your whole life, even though you've just met?

LUCAS. The day you were born.

RHIANNON. But then there are people you've been around forever, but you have no idea who they are. *(Losing her breath.)* You pass each other every day, your feet touch the same ground, but the air you breathe is so different, you shouldn't both be allowed to call yourselves human beings. *(Rhiannon breathes into her inhaler. Lucas wraps his arms around her.)*

LUCAS. Breathe, baby. Just breathe. Just this one breath, just this one exhale. Just this one breath, just this one exhale, just this one breath. *(Alice sets down the inflated globe and quietly leaves the room.)*

MOVEMENT TWELVE

Bashir's motel room. Alice approaches Bashir.

ALICE. You should not have spoken to my daughter.

BASHIR. What is so hard about facing your child and telling her who you are?

ALICE. Spoken like a true absentee father.

BASHIR. All those days you were in my face, sizing me up — I was there too. Watching you. Noticing things.

ALICE. I was a highly trained interrogator. Everything you saw was an act.

BASHIR. But what about your involuntary responses? The things you can't control. I know that when something excites you, your pupils dilate. I know your right eyelid twitches when you've had too much caffeine. I know all the different ways you sweat. I know everything that's true for you lives in what you're not saying.

ALICE. I was playing a role.

BASHIR. Sometimes a role resurrects things you killed off as a child because other people said they were wrong.

ALICE. You want me inside you. You think it will make you feel whole. You hope that if you hurt me enough, you can forget me.

BASHIR. When you were hard — when you screamed, ordered boards and chains — that was simple. I could go somewhere else. But when you were soft — when you touched my ears, my neck — my body had a will of its own. My own flesh, my own muscle, betrayed me.

ALICE. I'm a hepatitis carrier.

BASHIR. What?

ALICE. I went on suppressants when I had Rhiannon so she wouldn't get sick.

BASHIR. You're a carrier?

ALICE. I can't save you.

BASHIR. So I will die.

ALICE. I'm so sorry.

BASHIR. And what will happen to you?

ALICE. I don't know.

BASHIR. Will you stay in your glass house, forever punishing flowers?

ALICE. Stop. No more. Please.

BASHIR. *(Screaming.)* Stop. No more. Please. I swear I'm an innocent man. I don't know Osama or Saddam or Khalid. I was studying at a mosque. I just wanted to be a good Muslim. Please, I beg you. Believe me. *(Bashir pulls a black plastic bag out of his pocket. It is the same one he wore in the florist shop. He drops it on the floor. Taunting Alice. He locks eyes with her. With great desire and need.)* Please. *(Alice freezes. A long silence, as she battles something inside her.)*

ALICE. Shut up. Shut up! Don't you dare say a word unless you're spoken to, you stupid, sniveling son of a bitch. Listen carefully. If you don't do exactly what I say, I swear I will find your family and dump them into the sea. Nod if you understand me. *(Bashir nods. A strange peace fills his face.)* Drop to your hands and knees. Now crawl. Go! There's a plastic bag by your feet. Pull the bag over your head and bend forward at the waist, so that — *(Alice pauses as, without being asked, Bashir relaxes into the corresponding stress position.)* Look at that. You already know how I like it. Was this our favorite position? Did we do this for hours? Was I loud? Sweaty? Did you whimper? When I was done, did we share a cigarette? *(Horrified.)* Did I feel like I feel right now, absolutely amazing?

MOVEMENT THIRTEEN

Rhiannon is in her bedroom wearing the army jacket and interrogating the jumpsuit. Lucas is doing tai chi in the living room.

RHIANNON. Are you now, or have you ever been, a member of Al Qaeda? Do you know Khalid Sheik Muhammad? Muhammad Atta? Are you a Taliban? Where's Osama? *(Alice enters the living room.)*
LUCAS. *(To Alice.)* Remember when I broke my nose on our honeymoon? It wasn't from falling out of bed.
ALICE. What do you mean?
LUCAS. One night I woke up and you weren't there. I found you in the dining room, screaming at an empty chair. I called your name, but you were asleep. I touched your shoulder, and you whirled around with this look — and you broke my nose.
RHIANNON. *(Softly, to jumpsuit.)* If you were a bird, which would you be? Where would you fly for the winter?
ALICE. Why did you keep that from me?
LUCAS. You changed, Alice. So much. Even the way you kissed was different. It was like you were searching for something you could never find with me.
ALICE. You're enough. You've always been enough.
LUCAS. You know how you're supposed to act and react in every situation, but it's been lifetimes since something has moved you.
ALICE. You don't understand. You never have.
LUCAS. You went to war. You got back. You went to sleep. We're dust, Alice. Dead stars. We stopped giving off light lifetimes ago, but it's taken this long for anyone to notice.

ALICE. We're going to start over, okay? Another new leaf. It's like you said — we can get through anything if we still want the same thing. Do we?

RHIANNON. If your life was a fairy tale, which would it be? Would you live happily ever after?

LUCAS. No, Alice. We don't. We've never wanted the same thing.

ALICE. No, Lucas. Don't say that. You can't say that. *(Rhiannon makes blackout goggles out of a diving mask and duct tape. Bashir enters the living room.)*

BASHIR. I thought Americans had seven locks on their doors, and guns to guard them from men like me.

LUCAS. Who the fuck are you?

BASHIR. But maybe you need us to hold mirrors to your monstrosities.

LUCAS. I asked you a question.

RHIANNON. Is there a person who has changed the course of your life? Who were they, and what did they do?

BASHIR. You must be Lucas. According to your wife, we could be cousins.

LUCAS. Get out of my house!

ALICE. Lucas. Don't raise your voice.

LUCAS. Are you defending this man?

ALICE. It's not that simple.

LUCAS. Yes, it is. It's called a front door. It separates this family from the rest of the world, and if someone wants to cross that barrier, they knock. It's that simple. Whatever you two need to settle happens on the other side of that door. You do not bring your mess into our house.

ALICE. But I'm the mess, Lucas. Should I stay on the other side of that door too?

BASHIR. Your wife raped me. She didn't knock, she didn't ask for permission. She just came into my house.

RHIANNON. *(Softly.)* What do you dream about?

LUCAS. Alice, if there is any truth in what he's saying, you better speak up right now.

ALICE. I don't know.

RHIANNON. *(Whispering.)* What do you dream about?

BASHIR. The room was empty except for my chair. I felt her breath on my ears, my eyes, my neck. Ever since I was a boy, whenever someone whispered into my ear, I became … hard. It began in my toes. Something hot, boiling. I thought of every prophet. I whispered every prayer. I knew what would happen and so — I pretended she was my wife. And because I wished it, it became true. Somewhere around that time my wife stopped waiting for me. Shemayah left Zakiyah at my brother's house, put rocks in her pockets, and walked into the sea. *(To Alice.)* Now when I try to remember her face, it's only yours I see. *(Lucas picks up the inflated globe.)*

LUCAS. "My name is Alice. This is my globe. Before I am old I will know all these places." Did it work? Do you know the world, Alice? Do you understand everything?

ALICE. I know less, Lucas. Every day I live, I know less.

LUCAS. Rhiannon!

ALICE. Don't do this.

RHIANNON. *(From the bedroom.)* What, Dad? I'm busy.

LUCAS. Come here for a minute, baby. Your mom has something she wants to tell you. *(To Alice.)* If you want to turn over a new leaf, start with our daughter. Tell her who he is. *(Beat.)* Rhiannon! — *(Rhiannon enters.)*

RHIANNON. *(To Bashir.)* What are you doing here?

ALICE. Rhiannon, I think you've already met Bashir. He was a detainee at Guantánamo. One I interrogated.

RHIANNON. *(To Bashir.)* You lied to me?

BASHIR. You heard what you needed to. *(Rhiannon punches Bashir in the stomach. When he falls to the ground, Rhiannon kicks him in the face.)*

ALICE. Rhiannon! *(Lucas restrains Rhiannon. She tries to get away.)*

RHIANNON. *(To Bashir.)* I'm going to drown you in liquid nitrogen, then smash you into a billion pieces, so you have no way of becoming unburied.

ALICE. Rhiannon, don't say that. You're acting crazy.

RHIANNON. Then what am I allowed to say?

LUCAS. Whatever you need to, Rhiannon. Say whatever you need.

RHIANNON. *(To Bashir.)* Our fingernails are the same shape. They're not square like my dad's or stubby like my mom's. They're ovals, with perfect crescents. *(Blood streams out of Bashir's nose, covering his hands and face.)*

ALICE. He's bleeding. Both of you — stay away. *(Alice cradles Bashir in her arms and pinches his nose shut. She gets covered with his blood.)* Keep your head tilted. Does your nose feel broken? *(Bashir struggles to get away from Alice. Alice restrains him. Bashir spits in Alice's face. Alice turns away from Bashir to wipe off her face.)*

BASHIR. Why did you make me *(Hiccup.)* beg for something you could never give me?

ALICE. I'll stay with you.

LUCAS. Really?

ALICE. He has a few months, Lucas. He could stay with me for that long, couldn't he?

LUCAS. He could stay in a hospital, Alice. With people who know how to take care of him. Or do you know better than them what a dying man needs?

ALICE. *(Laughing.)* Yes, Lucas. I do. *(Helplessly.)* I do.

RHIANNON. *(To Bashir.)* You got the hiccups.

BASHIR. Zakiyah. *(Hiccup.)* Is that you?

RHIANNON. Has an elf crawled up your nose to do back-handsprings down your spine? Does your body know something your mind isn't ready to accept? *(Bashir holds out his hands. They flap in front of him.)*

BASHIR. *(To Rhiannon.)* Look, my angel, look — *(Hiccups. Rhiannon screams and lunges at Bashir. His hiccups stop. Alice looks back and forth between Rhiannon and Bashir. At their eyes. She moans, finally making a connection.)*

ALICE. Oh my God. Oh my God. Rhiannon — *(Alice reaches for Rhiannon, then stops herself, realizing her hands are covered in blood.)* Oh my God. Oh — baby.

RHIANNON. You never want me to understand. You never want me to know anything. *(Rhiannon runs to her room.)*

ALICE. Lucas. Their eyes. Their eyes are the same.

LUCAS. I don't care who you did or didn't fuck in a place nobody even remembers. Being a father is a commitment. Being a father is a choice. Rhiannon is my daughter. I raised her. *(Bashir reaches towards the direction of Rhiannon's exit.)*

BASHIR. I'm changing into a bird, my child. The one from our stories.

MOVEMENT FOURTEEN

In a hospital room, Riva checks Bashir's vitals. In her bedroom, Rhiannon wears the blackout goggles.

RIVA. Breathe in. Breathe out. In, and out. One more time. In, and out. Make a fist. Release. Other hand. Release. Lovely.

BASHIR. *(Realization.)* I left them for a faraway place because I thought it would make me feel whole. Allah was in my wife and daughter. Allah was in every person in my family. But I left them. For a mosque. In Afghanistan.

RIVA. You are in an American hospital. You don't have to explain anything.

BASHIR. I was farsighted. Allah was all around me, but too close for me to see. *(Bashir reaches for Riva's hands. She lets him hold them. In the living room. Alice stares into the inflated globe. Lucas cleans blood off the floor.)*

ALICE. It's just a crush. A stupid fourteen-year-old crush. She'll forget about him. She just needs time. It doesn't have to mean anything.

LUCAS. She knows. Not in her head yet, but every other part of her knows. We have to tell her the truth.

ALICE. What exactly do you want me to tell her, Lucas? That I raped a man then forgot about it, and that's why she exists? What is a fourteen-year-old girl going to do with that kind of truth? *(Rhiannon enters carrying the jumpsuit and blackout goggles. Lucas continues scrubbing the floor.)*

RHIANNON. Hey, Mom?

ALICE. Yes, baby?

RHIANNON. Will you drive me to the hospital?

ALICE. Are you hurt?

RHIANNON. I want to apologize to Bashir.

ALICE. It's not a good time, sweetheart. He's really sick.

RHIANNON. I need to ask him something.

ALICE. Whatever you need to ask him — ask me. I promise I will answer as honestly as I can.

RHIANNON. Forget it.

ALICE. Are you sure?

RHIANNON. Yeah. It's nothing.

ALICE. You know you're my girl, right? You know I'll do anything for you. Anything.

RHIANNON. Why do I feel like this about him?

ALICE. I don't know, but I swear to you that with time, this will hurt less. Can you trust me on this? *(Lucas puts away his towel and exits the house.)*

RHIANNON. Yeah, Mom. Sure thing.

ALICE. Anything else you'd like to ask me?

RHIANNON. I don't think so. 'Night, Mom.

ALICE. Night, baby. *(Rhiannon goes to her room. Alice exits the house, hugging the inflated globe. At the hospital, Bashir gasps and moans with pain. Riva stands by his side.)*

RIVA. I called Zakiyah. She's coming.

BASHIR. I don't want her to see me like this.

RIVA. There is nothing I wouldn't give for another day with my father.

BASHIR. What would you say?

RIVA. I wouldn't waste time with words. We would sit someplace sunny, and smile and cry and drink tea. *(Bashir holds out his Koran for Riva.)*

BASHIR. Pray for me.

RIVA. I haven't spoken Arabic since I was a little girl.

BASHIR. A terrible thing happened to your father. That doesn't make an entire language wrong.

RIVA. I can't. I'm so sorry.

BASHIR. Pretend, for a minute, that I am your father and that these words will put an end to his torture. Pretend they will bring him some peace. *(Riva takes the Koran and reads Bashir Surah 114, "Mankind." Her Arabic is rusty and hesitant at first, each word filling her with memories she has spent a lifetime repressing. As she reads, she grows more confident and compassionate.)*

RIVA.

Bismillaah ar-Rahman ar-Raheem
Qul a'uudhi bi rabbin naas
Malikin naas Ilaahin naas
Min sharril wawaasil khannas
Alladhee yuwaswisu fee suduurin naas
Minal Jinnati wa naas.

(She repeats it. In her bedroom, Rhiannon puts on the jumpsuit. She sets her inhaler and handcuffs key beside her. She puts on the blackout goggles. She handcuffs her hands. She tries a stress position.)

RHIANNON. Just. This. One. Breath. Just. This. One. Exhale. Just. This. One. Breath. Just. This. One. Exhale. *(Riva continues to read from the Koran. Bashir joins in. Lucas paces in the florist's shop, craving a fix. He tries to center himself through tai chi.)*

LUCAS. Bring your awareness to the sensations of contact wherever your body is being supported. Gently explore how this really feels. Become aware of your body's movements during breathing, at the chest and at the abdomen. *(Alice walks outside, hugging the globe. Rhiannon falls, accidentally kicking the key and the inhaler away. She doesn't notice. She resumes the stress position.)* Allow yourself simply to breathe, without trying to change or control your breath; just notice the sensations that go with every movement. As soon as you notice your mind wandering, bring your awareness gently back to the movement of the abdomen. Do this over and over again. Be patient with yourself.

RHIANNON and LUCAS. Just. This. One. Breath. Just. This. One. Exhale. Just. This. One. Breath. Just. This. One. Exhale.

ALICE. *(Simultaneously, remembering herself as a young girl.)* My name is Alice. This is my globe. Before I am old I will know all these places. *(Remembering herself as a soldier.)* My name is Alice. This is my globe. Before I am old I will know all these places. *(Seeing herself as she is now.)* My name is Alice. This is my globe. Before I am old I will know all these places. *(Rhiannon has an asthma attack. She feels around for the key to her handcuffs. She can't find it.)*

RHIANNON. I want this. I love this. I'm happy. I love this. I want this, I ... I ... *(Panicking, Rhiannon bangs her feet and arms on the ground, trying to be heard. She thrashes and flops violently on the floor, like a fish out of water.)* Help! Help. I can't breathe. I can't breathe. I can't breathe. Mommy ... *(Rhiannon dies. Bashir goes comatose. Riva stops reading from the Koran. A long stillness.)*

LUCAS. Bring awareness back to your whole body, sitting in the room. Open your eyes. Be ready for whatever is next. *(Lucas lifts Rhiannon's body and carries it offstage.)*

MOVEMENT FIFTEEN

Alice enters Bashir's hospital room. She hugs the inflated globe. Bashir lies in a hospital bed. Rhiannon's body.

ALICE. Can I see her? *(Bashir lifts his shirt up, revealing a large bandage on his abdomen. Alice's hands flutter towards Bashir's abdomen.)*
BASHIR. You can touch me. *(Alice touches the area around the bandage.)*
ALICE. Hey, Rhiannon. It's Mom. You're going to live with Bashir now. We'll stay in touch. Write emails, maybe call sometimes. *(Beat.)* I want you to know — I need you to know that — Rhiannon likes chicken soup on rainy days, her eggs sunny side up, and her hamburgers well-done. We go to the skate park every Sunday, but never before noon. She's allergic to tomatoes, and pretends to be allergic to honey. She thinks it's weird humans eat the pee of bees. She has asthma attacks in the winter so we keep an inhaler by her pillow. She gets three extra candles on her birthday cake. One for the year gone by, one for the years to come, and one for the year she's living. It has to be a strawberry shortcake. With Cool Whip instead of whipped cream.
BASHIR. I belong to you.
ALICE. You have what you came for. More life. Don't waste it.
BASHIR. What will you do now?
ALICE. *(Motions to inflated globe in her arms.)* All I know is that — she's in here. She's still in here. This is her breath.
BASHIR. Stay with me.
ALICE. I can't. I shouldn't. *(Alice exits.)*
BASHIR. I want this. *(Tries, and fails to take a deep breath.)* I love this. *(Tries again.)* I'm happy. *(Another attempt. Outside the hospital room, Alice unfastens the nozzle of the globe.)*
ALICE. Just. This. One. Breath. *(Alice inhales air from the globe.)*
BASHIR. I love this. I want this. I … I …
ALICE. Just. This. One. Exhale. *(Alice exhales. She continues breathing in the globe through the next scene. Zakiyah enters the hospital room, wearing an orange scarf. She is played by the actress play-*

ing Riva.)

BASHIR. Shemayah. I thought that with my new liver, my hallucinations would end.

ZAKIYAH. My mother is dead.

ALICE. *(Softly.)* Just. This. One. Breath.

BASHIR. Zakiyah?

ZAKIYAH. You don't look like my father.

BASHIR. Interrogate me.

ALICE. *(Softly.)* Just. This. One. Exhale.

ZAKIYAH. What did you serve me chai in?

BASHIR. The cracked blue bowl we kept by the window.

ZAKIYAH. How many stories did you read each night before I would sleep?

BASHIR. You hated bedtime stories. You only wanted to hear my weekly weather prophecies.

ZAKIYAH. What's the last thing you said to me?

BASHIR. The last time I saw you, you wore a striped shirt and yellow pants. I kissed your head and said, "Have a good day at school. I'll see you in a few weeks."

ALICE. *(Softly.)* Just. This. One. Breath.

ZAKIYAH. It's really you. At last!

BASHIR. Everything I did in prison, to survive, was for you. For this moment.

ZAKIYAH. Your nightmare has ended. The happiness can begin.

BASHIR. I dreamed of this moment. So many times. I thought it was all that I needed. I wanted you back. I wanted you so much.

ZAKIYAH. I'm here. You will come back to Pakistan. We will never be separated again.

BASHIR. I'm sorry. I'm so sorry.

ZAKIYAH. Rest now, *abba*. Take as much time as you need. When you are feeling stronger, I will take you home.

BASHIR. I can't go back.

ZAKIYAH. I don't understand. You don't want me?

BASHIR. Oh. My angel. I don't deserve you.

ZAKIYAH. I came for my father. I came here to get you.

BASHIR. Your father died in prison.

ZAKIYAH. Then bring him back to life.

ALICE. *(Softly.)* Just. This. One. Exhale.

BASHIR. I thought I could. I tried, so many times. But the only way I kept from going crazy was by making myself love what they

44

did to me.

ZAKIYAH. Everything that has happened before this moment I can forgive. You were in prison. You couldn't get a visa. You were sick. But you are no longer in prison. You have a visa. You're not sick. If you don't come with me now, I will never forgive you. I will forget I ever had a father.

BASHIR. I go home and then what? You will expect me to be normal in a month. To smile and act happy. For a week people will be curious. What happened to Bashir? How did he become so strange? Then, after a short time, no one will listen to the ravings of a broken man. Why should they?

ALICE. *(Softly.)* Just. This. One. Breath.

ZAKIYAH. Please, *abba*, come home! *(Zakiyah reaches for Bashir. He pushes her away.)*

BASHIR. Go home, Zakiyah. Forget me.

ALICE. *(Softly.)* Just. This. One. Exhale. *(Zakiyah takes a deep breath. She regains her composure. She smiles as brightly as she can.)*

ZAKIYAH. Forgive me, Father, for raising my voice. You don't mean what you've been saying. Soon your new liver will eliminate the toxins that have poisoned your body, and everything you're thinking will change.

BASHIR. I need Alice. *(Bashir struggles to get out of bed. Zakiyah restrains him.)*

ZAKIYAH. Close your eyes, *abba*. Dream and get well.

BASHIR. Please, Zakiyah. Bring me Alice.

ZAKIYAH. When you're ready, I'll take you home. You'll heal. Everything will be new again. You'll see.

ALICE. *(Softly.)* Just. This. One. Breath. *(Alice sucks the remaining air from the globe. It crumples at her lips. She starts to leave the stage, then stops when she hears:)*

BASHIR. Alice! *(Alice enters the hospital room and approaches Bashir. He looks away from Zakiyah and meets Alice's gaze. Electricity crackles between them. They stare at each other as the lights crescendo to full, blinding brightness, then fade to black.)*

End of Play

PROPERTY LIST

Asthma inhaler
Headphones
Lighter
Recorder
Notebook
Photo
Bottle of pills
Piece of paper
Lipstick
Cake, frosting
Inflatable globe
Yellow roses
Black plastic bag
Printout
Money
Notepad, pen
Orange jumpsuit wrapped in brown paper
Backpack
Phone
Army jacket
Tripod with digital camera
Diving goggles covered with duct tape
Bucket, sponge
Koran
Handcuffs, key

SOUND EFFECTS

Ocean, white noise
Woman singing

NEW PLAYS

★ **BENGAL TIGER AT THE BAGHDAD ZOO by Rajiv Joseph.** The lives of two American Marines and an Iraqi translator are forever changed by an encounter with a quick-witted tiger who haunts the streets of war-torn Baghdad. "[A] boldly imagined, harrowing and surprisingly funny drama." –*NY Times.* "Tragic yet darkly comic and highly imaginative." –*CurtainUp.* [5M, 2W] ISBN: 978-0-8222-2565-2

★ **THE PITMEN PAINTERS by Lee Hall, inspired by a book by William Feaver.** Based on the triumphant true story, a group of British miners discover a new way to express themselves and unexpectedly become art-world sensations. "Excitingly ambiguous, in-the-moment theater." –*NY Times.* "Heartfelt, moving and deeply politicized." –*Chicago Tribune.* [5M, 2W] ISBN: 978-0-8222-2507-2

★ **RELATIVELY SPEAKING by Ethan Coen, Elaine May and Woody Allen.** In TALKING CURE, Ethan Coen uncovers the sort of insanity that can only come from family. Elaine May explores the hilarity of passing in GEORGE IS DEAD. In HONEYMOON MOTEL, Woody Allen invites you to the sort of wedding day you won't forget. "Firecracker funny." –*NY Times.* "A rollicking good time." –*New Yorker.* [8M, 7W] ISBN: 978-0-8222-2394-8

★ **SONS OF THE PROPHET by Stephen Karam.** If to live is to suffer, then Joseph Douaihy is more alive than most. With unexplained chronic pain and the fate of his reeling family on his shoulders, Joseph's health, sanity, and insurance premium are on the line. "Explosively funny." –*NY Times.* "At once deep, deft and beautifully made." –*New Yorker.* [5M, 3W] ISBN: 978-0-8222-2597-3

★ **THE MOUNTAINTOP by Katori Hall.** A gripping reimagination of events the night before the assassination of the civil rights leader Dr. Martin Luther King, Jr. "An ominous electricity crackles through the opening moments." –*NY Times.* "[A] thrilling, wild, provocative flight of magical realism." –*Associated Press.* "Crackles with theatricality and a humanity more moving than sainthood." –*NY Newsday.* [1M, 1W] ISBN: 978-0-8222-2603-1

★ **ALL NEW PEOPLE by Zach Braff.** Charlie is 35, heartbroken, and just wants some time away from the rest of the world. Long Beach Island seems to be the perfect escape until his solitude is interrupted by a motley parade of misfits who show up and change his plans. "Consistently and sometimes sensationally funny." –*NY Times.* "A morbidly funny play about the trendy new existential condition of being young, adorable, and miserable." –*Variety.* [2M, 2W] ISBN: 978-0-8222-2562-1

DRAMATISTS PLAY SERVICE, INC.
440 Park Avenue South, New York, NY 10016 212-683-8960 Fax 212-213-1539
postmaster@dramatists.com   www.dramatists.com

NEW PLAYS

★ **CLYBOURNE PARK by Bruce Norris.** WINNER OF THE 2011 PULITZER PRIZE AND 2012 TONY AWARD. Act One takes place in 1959 as community leaders try to stop the sale of a home to a black family. Act Two is set in the same house in the present day as the now predominantly African-American neighborhood battles to hold its ground. "Vital, sharp-witted and ferociously smart." –*NY Times.* "A theatrical treasure…Indisputably, uproariously funny." –*Entertainment Weekly.* [4M, 3W] ISBN: 978-0-8222-2697-0

★ **WATER BY THE SPOONFUL by Quiara Alegría Hudes.** WINNER OF THE 2012 PULITZER PRIZE. A Puerto Rican veteran is surrounded by the North Philadelphia demons he tried to escape in the service. "This is a very funny, warm, and yes uplifting play." –*Hartford Courant.* "The play is a combination poem, prayer and app on how to cope in an age of uncertainty, speed and chaos." –*Variety.* [4M, 3W] ISBN: 978-0-8222-2716-8

★ **RED by John Logan.** WINNER OF THE 2010 TONY AWARD. Mark Rothko has just landed the biggest commission in the history of modern art. But when his young assistant, Ken, gains the confidence to challenge him, Rothko faces the agonizing possibility that his crowning achievement could also become his undoing. "Intense and exciting." –*NY Times.* "Smart, eloquent entertainment." –*New Yorker.* [2M] ISBN: 978-0-8222-2483-9

★ **VENUS IN FUR by David Ives.** Thomas, a beleaguered playwright/director, is desperate to find an actress to play Vanda, the female lead in his adaptation of the classic sadomasochistic tale *Venus in Fur.* "Ninety minutes of good, kinky fun." –*NY Times.* "A fast-paced journey into one man's entrapment by a clever, vengeful female." –*Associated Press.* [1M, 1W] ISBN: 978-0-8222-2603-1

★ **OTHER DESERT CITIES by Jon Robin Baitz.** Brooke returns home to Palm Springs after a six-year absence and announces that she is about to publish a memoir dredging up a pivotal and tragic event in the family's history—a wound they don't want reopened. "Leaves you feeling both moved and gratifyingly sated." –*NY Times.* "A genuine pleasure." –*NY Post.* [2M, 3W] ISBN: 978-0-8222-2605-5

★ **TRIBES by Nina Raine.** Billy was born deaf into a hearing family and adapts brilliantly to his family's unconventional ways, but it's not until he meets Sylvia, a young woman on the brink of deafness, that he finally understands what it means to be understood. "A smart, lively play." –*NY Times.* "[A] bright and boldly provocative drama." –*Associated Press.* [3M, 2W] ISBN: 978-0-8222-2751-9

DRAMATISTS PLAY SERVICE, INC.
440 Park Avenue South, New York, NY 10016 212-683-8960 Fax 212-213-1539
postmaster@dramatists.com www.dramatists.com